A yummy snacks for kids cookbook is a fun and playful collection of recipes designed to appeal to young taste buds and inspire creativity in the kitchen. This type of cookbook is specifically geared towards parents, caregivers, and children who want to explore new flavors and textures while also making healthy and delicious snacks that are easy to prepare.

The recipes in a yummy snacks for kids cookbook are typically organized by categories such as sweet, savory, crunchy, chewy, and more. Each recipe includes a list of ingredients, clear and simple instructions, and colorful photographs of the finished snacks. Many of these cookbooks also include helpful tips for getting kids involved in the cooking process, such as letting them measure and mix ingredients, decorate the snacks, or choose their own flavor combinations.

Pineapple Green Smoothie

INGREDIENTS:

1 CUP ALMOND MILK
1 CUP FROZEN PINEAPPLE CHUNKS
2 HANDFULS FRESH SPINACH
1 SCOOP VANILLA PROTEIN

This smoothie is perfect for kids and adults alike! It's a great way to get the benefits of healthy greens while still enjoying a delicious treat. The combination of pineapple, almond milk, spinach, and vanilla protein make this smoothie both healthy and tasty. Plus, it's easy to prepare in just minutes.

To make this smoothie, start by adding one cup of almond milk to your blender. Next, add in one cup of frozen pineapple chunks and two handfuls of fresh spinach. Finally, scoop in one scoop of vanilla protein. Blend all the ingredients together until smooth.

Enjoy your smoothie as a snack or as part of a meal! You can even add a few extras like chia seeds or flaxseeds to make this smoothie even more nutritious. Adding smoothies to your diet is an easy way to get the vitamins and minerals you need while also enjoying something delicious.

Whether you're looking for smoothie recipes for kids or just trying to lead a healthier lifestyle, this pineapple green smoothie is a great option. With just five ingredients and no added sugar, you can have a healthy smoothie in minutes. Enjoy!

Lemon Tart

Ingredients:

For the pastry crust:

1 1/2 cups all-purpose flour
1/2 cup unsalted butter, chilled and cubed
1/4 cup confectioners' sugar
1 large egg yolk
2 tablespoons ice water

For the lemon filling:

1 tablespoon lemon zest (1 lemon's worth)
1/2 cup lemon juice (from 1 - 2 lemons)
3/4 cup white sugar
12 tablespoons (170g) unsalted butter, cut into 1cm (1/2") cubes
3 whole large eggs
3 large egg yolks

Instructions:

To make the pastry crust, place the flour, butter, and confectioners' sugar in a food processor and pulse until the mixture resembles coarse breadcrumbs. Add the egg yolk and ice water and pulse until the dough comes together.
Turn the dough out onto a lightly floured surface and knead briefly until smooth. Flatten into a disk, wrap in plastic wrap, and refrigerate for 30 minutes.
Preheat the oven to 350°F (180°C).
Roll out the pastry on a lightly floured surface and use to line a 9-inch (23cm) tart tin with a removable bottom. Prick the base with a fork and refrigerate for 15 minutes.
Line the pastry case with baking paper and fill with baking beads or uncooked rice. Bake for 10 minutes, then remove the paper and beads and bake for a further 5 minutes, or until lightly golden.
To make the lemon filling, place the lemon zest, lemon juice, sugar, and butter in a heatproof bowl set over a saucepan of simmering water (making sure the bowl doesn't touch the water). Stir until the butter has melted and the mixture is smooth.
Whisk together the eggs and egg yolks in a separate bowl. Gradually whisk in the lemon mixture.
Pour the lemon filling into the pastry case and bake for 20-25 minutes, or until the filling is just set. Allow to cool to room temperature before serving.
Enjoy your delicious lemon tart!

Chocolate Almond Cups

INGREDIENTS
1 HEAPING CUP VEGAN, REFINED SUGAR-FREE DARK CHOCOLATE
1 TABLESPOON COCONUT OIL.
½ CUP RAW CREAMY UNSALTED ALMOND BUTTER*
¼ CUP SUPERFINE BLANCHED ALMOND FLOUR.
2 TABLESPOON MAPLE SYRUP.
PINCH OF SALT.

Preparing these delicious Sugar Free Chocolate Almond Cups is a breeze. All you need to do is melt the vegan, refined sugar-free dark chocolate with the coconut oil, stirring until smooth and creamy. Then, spoon about 1 teaspoon of the melted chocolate into each cupcake liner. Top with a teaspoon of almond butter and sprinkle with almond flour. Repeat until all the cups are filled. Finally, drizzle each cup with a little of the maple syrup and sprinkle with a pinch of salt. Put in the refrigerator for at least 2 hours before serving.

These Sugar Free Chocolate Almond Cups make for a healthy dessert option that is no sugar but still just as delicious. They satisfy your sweet craving without compromising on flavor. With the simple ingredients and minimal preparation, you can whip these up in no time for an instant treat! Enjoy!

*Note: If you're using salted almond butter, don't add any more salt before baking. The extra salt won't be necessary. replace the almond butter with your favorite nut butter to make it your own. You can also switch up the dark chocolate for milk or white chocolate.

Panna Cotta

INGREDIENTS

1 1/2 TSP. GELATIN POWDER (UNSWEETENED)
1/4 CUP WATER (COLD)
1/4 CUP WATER (BOILING)
2 CUPS HEAVY CREAM.
2 TSP. VANILLA EXTRACT.
SUGAR SUBSTITUTE, SUCH AS STEVIA, EQUAL TO 1/4 CUP SUGAR.
PINCH OF SALT.

If you're looking for a no sugar, healthy dessert recipe that is easy to make and delicious, then this panna cotta recipe is the perfect choice. It's made with no sugar added, using a sugar substitute like stevia or equal in place of traditional white sugar. The ingredients are simple and straightforward - just gelatin powder, cold and boiling water, heavy cream, vanilla extract, sugar substitute, and a pinch of salt. The end result is a light and creamy no sugar dessert that everyone in the family will love. So go ahead and give this no sugar panna cotta recipe a try - you won't be disappointed!

This no sugar panna cotta recipe is easy to whip up and makes a great dessert for any occasion. It's light and creamy with no added sugar, so you can enjoy it guilt-free. Plus, it only takes about 10 minutes of prep time! For best results, make sure your gelatin powder is unsweetened and use the recommended amounts of cold and boiling water. For a no sugar dessert, you'll want to use a sugar substitute like stevia or equal in place of traditional white sugar. Finally, add a pinch of salt for added flavor and sweetness.

Strawberry Cheesecake Smoothie

INGREDIENTS
2 CUPS STRAWBERRIES, SLICED
¾ CUP RAW UNSALTED CASHEWS
1 CUP ALMOND MILK
½ FROZEN BANANA
2 TABLESPOONS LEMON JUICE
1 CUP ICE

This smoothie is perfect for kids – it's healthy and delicious! Preparation of this smoothie couldn't be easier. All you need to do is blend together the strawberries, cashews, almond milk, banana, lemon juice and ice until smooth. Pour your smoothie into a glass and enjoy!

This smoothie recipe is both healthy and delicious, perfect for kids of all ages. Not only that, it's easy to make with only a few simple ingredients! So next time you're looking for a smoothie recipe your kids will love, try out this Strawberry Cheesecake Smoothie. They won't be disappointed!

Enjoy!

Rice Chocolate Pudding

Ingredients
1/3 cup medium-grain rice.
1/4 cup cocoa powder.
3 1/4 cups skim milk.
1/4 cup caster sugar.
canned pears, to serve.

Here's the method to go along with the ingredients:

Rinse the rice and place it in a medium-sized saucepan with 1 1/2 cups of water. Bring to a boil, then reduce the heat to low and simmer for 15 minutes, or until the rice is cooked and the water has been absorbed.
Add the cocoa powder, milk and sugar to the saucepan and stir to combine. Place the pan over medium heat and cook for 10-15 minutes, stirring frequently, until the pudding thickens and the rice is very tender.
Divide the pudding between four serving dishes and chill in the fridge for at least 1 hour, or until set. Serve the pudding with canned pears on top. Enjoy!

Chocolate Avocado Mousse

Avocado and chocolate mousse is a delicious no sugar dessert recipe that is also healthy. To make this decadent treat, you will need two ripe avocados chopped, 200g of good quality dark eating chocolate (60-75% cocoa) broken into pieces, ½ cup of your preferred milk of choice such as cow's, almond or coconut milk, and two tablespoons of liquid honey or pure maple syrup (optional).

To prepare the mousse, first melt the chocolate in a heatproof bowl over simmering water or in a microwave. Once melted, set aside to cool slightly. In a food processor combine the avocados and stir with melted chocolate until combined and smooth. Add milk and sweetener of choice to the mixture and blend together until light and creamy.

Transfer the mousse into separate bowls or glasses, cover with cling film, and refrigerate for 1-2 hours. When ready to eat, enjoy - this delicious no sugar dessert recipe is guilt-free! Enjoy!

You can also serve the mousse with some fresh berries or grated dark chocolate for a touch of sweetness. No matter how you choose to enjoy your avocado and chocolate mousse, it definitely is a healthy dessert that will satisfy all taste buds! Enjoy!

OVERNIGHT OATS

Overnight oats are a great way to make sure your child's breakfast is ready when they wake up – just combine rolled oats, milk, and yogurt in a mason jar the night before and let it sit overnight. In the morning, you can add fresh fruit for extra flavor.

Pumpkin Pie

INGREDIENTS

1 (15-OUNCE) CAN PUMPKIN PUREE.
1 (12-OUNCE) CAN EVAPORATED MILK.
3 LARGE EGGS.
3/4 CUP GRANULATED ARTIFICIAL SWEETENER, SUCH AS SPLENDA OR TRUVIA.
1 TEASPOON GROUND CINNAMON.
1/2 TEASPOON GROUND GINGER.
1/4 TEASPOON GROUND NUTMEG.
1/4 TEASPOON SALT.

Pumpkin pie is a classic no sugar dessert recipe that can be enjoyed any time of the year. It's a healthy alternative to other high-sugar desserts, and it won't break the calorie bank. Preparing a pumpkin pie is easy with just a few simple steps.

First, preheat your oven to 350°F and grease a 9-inch pie pan.

In a large bowl, mix together 1 (15-ounce) can of pumpkin puree, 1 (12-ounce) can evaporated milk, 3 large eggs, 3/4 cup granulated artificial sweetener such as Splenda or Truvia, 1 teaspoon ground cinnamon, 1/2 teaspoon ground ginger, 1/4 teaspoon ground nutmeg, and 1/4 teaspoon salt. Whisk everything together until combined.

Pour the mixture into the prepared pie pan and bake for 50-55 minutes or until a knife inserted into the center of the pie comes out clean. Let cool before serving. Enjoy!

Almond Banana Muffins

INGREDIENTS

BANANA MUFFINS ULTRA-FINE ALMOND FLOUR –
SALT
BAKING POWDER OR USE 1 TEASPOON OF BAKING SODA INSTEAD.
CINNAMON
MASHED BANANAS – THE BEST ARE RIPE BANANAS TO ADD LOTS OF BANANA FLAVOR AND AVOID ADDING ANY SWEETENER IN THE RECIPE.
LARGE EGGS AT ROOM TEMPERATURE
COCONUT OIL OR MELTED BUTTER
VANILLA EXTRACT
STEVIA DROPS OR 1/3 CUP OF GRANULATED SWEETENER OF CHOICE

These muffins are so good, you won't even miss the sugar! ripe bananas add natural sweetness and moisture, while almond flour and coconut oil keep them tender and rich.

To make them, simply combine all of the ingredients in a bowl and mix until well combined. Then, spoon the batter into a muffin tin and bake at 350 degrees F for about 20 minutes.

These almond banana muffins are a delicious and healthy dessert option - perfect for those looking for no sugar dessert recipes! If you want to add more sweetness, you can always drizzle with honey or maple syrup. Enjoy!

Strawberry Toast

Strawberry Toast is a healthy and tasty breakfast option for kids that's easy to prepare. To make it, start by melting the butter in a medium-sized skillet over medium heat. Add the sliced strawberries and cook for 5 minutes or until the berries have softened. Next, add the maple syrup, orange zest, non-fat milk, and teaspoon of salt. Cook for another 3 minutes or until the mixture thickens. Finally, place the slices of cinnamon raisin bread in a single layer on top of the strawberry mixture. Crack three eggs over the toast and let cook until the whites are set and yolks have just started to become soft. Serve immediately with a sprinkle of extra orange zest. Enjoy!

Lemon Bars

Healthy Lemon Bars are an easy no-sugar dessert recipe that you can enjoy guilt-free. This delicious treat is made with just 5 simple ingredients and no added sugars, making it a healthy alternative to traditional sugary desserts. With its bright and zesty flavors of lemon juice and zest, this no sugar dessert will surely become a favorite.

To create this no-sugar dessert, start by combining all-purpose flour (or whole wheat or oat flour), butter (or solid coconut oil), granulated sweetener (erythritol, stevia, sugar) and eggs in a bowl until well blended. Press the mixture into a baking pan and bake at 350 degrees Fahrenheit for 20 minutes.

Once the base is baked, combine lemon juice and zest with an additional sweetener of your choice in a bowl and pour it over the top of the cooked layer. Bake for an additional 15 minutes and cool completely before cutting into bars. Serve chilled or at room temperature for a light, no sugar dessert that is sure to satisfy your sweet tooth. Enjoy!

Try this no-sugar dessert recipe today and indulge without the guilt of added sugars. Healthy Lemon Bars are a delicious way to satisfy your sweet cravings in a healthy and satisfying way. With its bright flavors and no added sugar, it's no wonder why this no sugar dessert is a favorite.

Try it today and let us know how you liked it! You won't be disappointed. Enjoy!

Chocolate Peanut Butter Banana Smoothie

INGREDIENTS

1 BANANA, FROZEN
1 CUP MILK OF CHOICE
¼ CUP OLD-FASHIONED ROLLED OATS
3 TABLESPOONS NATURAL PEANUT BUTTER*
1 TABLESPOON COCOA POWDER
CHOCOLATE CHIPS, FOR SERVING (OPTIONAL)

This smoothie recipe is a delicious, healthy treat for kids of all ages. It's easy to make and requires only 5 ingredients: banana, milk of choice, old-fashioned rolled oats, natural peanut butter, and cocoa powder.

To begin preparing the smoothie, take one frozen banana and chop it into small pieces before adding it to a blender. Next, add one cup of your preferred type of milk along with ¼ cup old-fashioned rolled oats, 3 tablespoons natural peanut butter, and 1 tablespoon cocoa powder. Blend until smooth and creamy.

As an optional step, you can also top the smoothie off with some chocolate chips for added sweetness and crunch. Serve immediately and enjoy!

This smoothie is a great way to get your kids to eat something healthy and delicious. For an added nutrient boost, you can also add some flaxseed or chia seeds into the smoothie as well. With five simple ingredients, it's quick and easy to make this smoothie recipe for kids. Enjoy!

Note: If using smooth peanut butter, you may need to add a bit more sweetener. Be sure to read the labels on your ingredients carefully and choose one that is free of added sugars or other unnecessary fillers.

Banana Chia Pudding

INGREDIENTS

2 LARGE OVERRIPE BANANAS.
2 CUPS UNSWEETENED COCONUT (BEVERAGE), ALMOND OR CASHEW MILK.
6 TABLESPOONS CHIA SEEDS.

Banana Chia Pudding is a no sugar dessert recipe that anyone can prepare in no time at all! It's healthy and delicious, making it the perfect treat for any occasion. To make this tasty no-sugar dessert, you'll need two overripe bananas, two cups of unsweetened coconut (beverage), almond or cashew milk, and six tablespoons of chia seeds. First, mash the bananas in a bowl until no lumps remain. Add the milk and stir to combine. Then add the chia seeds and stir again until everything is mixed together well. Cover the bowl with plastic wrap and place it in the refrigerator for a few hours or overnight. Once the chia pudding has thickened and all of the ingredients have blended together, you can enjoy it! Serve it with fresh fruit or your favorite topping. Banana Chia Pudding is a no sugar dessert recipe that's sure to satisfy any sweet tooth! Enjoy!

Peanut Butter Pancakes

Ingredients

250g crunchy peanut butter.
50g unsalted butter, cubed, plus extra for cooking.
6 tbsp maple syrup.
300g self-raising flour.
1 tsp baking powder.
1 tbsp golden caster sugar.
2 large eggs.
350ml milk.

1. In a medium saucepan, melt the peanut butter and butter over low-medium heat until completely combined.
2. Add in the maple syrup, stirring frequently until fully incorporated. Set aside to cool slightly.
3. Combine the flour, baking powder and sugar in a large bowl and stir to combine.
4. In a separate bowl whisk together the eggs and milk until light and frothy, then add this to the dry ingredients along with the cooled peanut butter mixture. Stir together until just combined; don't over mix as this will make your pancakes tough!
5. Heat a non-stick frying pan over medium heat and lightly grease

Yogurt Sorbet

Yogurt sorbet is a refreshing, no-sugar dessert that provides a healthy alternative to sugary treats. It's easy to prepare and requires only three ingredients: Greek yogurt, granulated sweetener of choice, and optional vanilla extract.

To make this delicious treat you'll need to start by combining the Greek yogurt with the sweetener of your choice in a bowl. Stir until the sugar is completely dissolved. Then, add the vanilla extract and stir again to combine.

Once all the ingredients are mixed together, spoon the mixture into an ice cream maker and follow the manufacturer's instructions to churn it into a frozen sorbet. Alternatively, you can pour the mixture into a freezer-safe container and freeze it for several hours, stirring occasionally to break up any ice crystals that form.

When you're ready to serve the sorbet, scoop it into bowls or glasses and enjoy! Since there's no added sugar, this healthy dessert is perfect for anyone looking to satisfy their sweet tooth without consuming too many calories. And, it's sure to please everyone in the family - even the pickiest of eaters!

Chocolate Bark

This no-sugar dessert is a great way to enjoy the holiday season without compromising on taste. It's a healthy, easy-to-make holiday bark that will satisfy your sweet tooth while keeping things light and healthy. Making this Sugar Free Chocolate Holiday Bark is simple and straightforward: all you need are two bags of sugar free chocolate chips, ½ teaspoon of vanilla extract, 1 cup of nuts, and up to 1 cup of dried fruit. For an extra kick, you can even add melted sugar free white chocolate, sugar free crushed candy canes or chopped pretzels. However you choose to make it, this no-sugar dessert will be sure to please the whole family! So next time you're looking for a no sugar dessert recipe to make for a holiday party or family gathering, consider this Sugar Free Chocolate Holiday Bark. With its simple ingredients and no-sugar taste, it is sure to be a hit! So gather your family and friends, whip up this no-sugar dessert, sit back and enjoy the holiday season!

Vanilla Honey Cupcakes

Are you looking for no sugar dessert recipes and healthy desserts? Look no further! These delicious vanilla honey cupcakes are the perfect way to satisfy your sweet tooth without relying on processed sugars. With just a few simple ingredients, you can easily whip up a batch of these scrumptious treats in no time.

To prepare, gather the following ingredients: 1 1/2 cups plain all purpose flour, 1/2 tsp baking soda, 1/2 tsp baking powder, 1/2 tsp salt, 1 tsp pure vanilla extract, 1/3 cup whole milk, 1/2 cup softened butter and 1/2 cup raw honey.

Once you have all your ingredients, preheat the oven to 350°F and line a cupcake tin with paper liners. In a medium-sized bowl, whisk together the flour, baking soda, baking powder and salt until no lumps remain. Set aside.

In a separate large bowl, cream together the butter, honey and vanilla using an electric mixer until light and fluffy. Add the milk and mix until fully combined. Slowly add in the dry ingredients, mixing until just incorporated.

Spoon the batter into the cupcake liners, filling each no more than 2/3 full. Bake for 18 to 20 minutes or until a toothpick inserted into one of the cupcakes comes out clean. Allow to cool completely before serving. Enjoy!

These delicious vanilla honey cupcakes are a great no sugar dessert option and make a perfect healthy dessert for your next gathering. With no processed sugars and simple ingredients, these cupcakes are sure to be a hit!

Happy baking! ☺

Berry Pancakes

INGREDIENTS

1 CUP ALL PURPOSE FLOUR.
2 TABLESPOONS BUTTER.
1 TEASPOON BAKING POWDER.
1/4 CUP BLUE BERRIES.
1 CUP MILK.
1 EGG.
BUTTER OR OIL FOR FRYING.

Berry pancakes are an incredibly delicious and healthy no sugar dessert recipe that can be prepared in just a few simple steps. To make them, start by whisking together the all-purpose flour, baking powder and butter in a bowl. Then mix in the blueberries and milk until everything is fully combined. Next, crack one egg into the mixture to give it an extra boost of flavor and nutrition. Lastly, heat up a pan with some butter or oil before adding small scoops of the batter in to fry. Serve these yummy berry pancakes hot and enjoy as a healthy dessert!
The end result is sure to satisfy any sweet tooth without all the added sugar. You can even top them with a fresh fruit like strawberries or raspberries for extra sweetness. Enjoy!

Chocolate Bread And Butter Pudding

Ingredients

40g unsalted butter, softened, plus extra for greasing the tin.
8 slices white bread, cut into medium slices (preferably 1 day old)
50g raisins & cranberries mix.
400ml whole milk.
50ml double cream.
1 x 100g bar dark chocolate (70% cocoa solids), roughly chopped.
75g caster sugar.
1 orange, zested.

Here are the instructions for making chocolate bread and butter pudding:

Preheat the oven to 180°C (160°C fan)/350°F/gas mark 4. Grease a 1.5-litre ovenproof dish with butter.

Spread the softened butter on one side of each slice of bread, then cut them into quarters.

Arrange half of the bread slices, buttered-side up, in the bottom of the prepared dish. Sprinkle half of the raisins and cranberries over the bread.

In a saucepan, gently heat the milk, cream, chocolate, sugar, and orange zest, stirring constantly until the chocolate has melted and the sugar has dissolved.

In a separate bowl, beat the eggs together. Pour the chocolate mixture over the eggs, whisking continuously.

Pour half of the chocolate custard mixture over the bread in the dish, then add the remaining bread slices, buttered-side up, and sprinkle over the remaining raisins and cranberries. Pour the remaining chocolate custard over the top.

Let the pudding sit for 15-20 minutes, so the bread absorbs some of the custard.

Place the dish in a roasting tin, then fill the tin with hot water until it comes halfway up the sides of the pudding dish.

Bake the pudding for 35-40 minutes or until it is set and the bread is golden brown.

Serve the bread and butter pudding warm with a dollop of whipped cream, if desired.

Pumpkin Banana Smoothie

1 CUP PUMPKIN PUREE. GREAT VALUE 100% PURE PUMPKIN, 15 OZ.
1 CUP MILK.
1 BANANA, SLICED.
2 TABLESPOONS BROWN SUGAR.
¼ TEASPOON GROUND CINNAMON.
¼ TEASPOON VANILLA EXTRACT.

This smoothie is a great way to introduce kids to healthy smoothies. It only takes minutes to make and it's full of nutrients that will keep them feeling energized and satisfied.

To prepare the smoothie, combine all ingredients in a blender and blend until smooth. If desired, add a few ice cubes for an extra thick smoothie. You can also top the smoothie with a dollop of whipped cream or sprinkle some cinnamon on top for extra flavor.

This smoothie is full of vitamins, minerals, and antioxidants that make it healthy and delicious. Pumpkin puree provides beta carotene and fiber, banana adds potassium to the smoothie, while the cinnamon and brown sugar add just a touch of sweetness.

This smoothie is sure to be a hit with kids and adults alike! Enjoy it as a healthy snack or even breakfast on the go. You can also freeze leftovers in popsicle molds for an extra special treat.

Happy blending!

Fruit Salad

Ingredients

4 cups fresh pineapple chunks.
1 qt. strawberries, hulled and sliced in half.
3 cups seedless green grapes.
2 mangoes, peeled and sliced.
2 (4-oz.) containers fresh raspberries.
2 cups Greek yogurt.
1 tablespoon dark brown sugar.
1 tablespoon honey.

Fruit salad is a great option for a healthy breakfast for kids. With the right ingredients, you can make a delicious and nutritious meal that everyone in your family will enjoy.

To make this fruit salad, start by combining the pineapple chunks, strawberries, green grapes, mangoes and raspberries in a large bowl. Stir to combine all of the fruits evenly. In a separate small bowl, mix together the Greek yogurt with dark brown sugar and honey until fully combined. Gently fold this mixture into the fruit until it is evenly distributed throughout. Refrigerate the salad for at least 30 minutes before serving so that all of the flavors have time to mingle together. Serve chilled or at room temperature as desired. Enjoy!

Vanilla Muffins

INGREDIENTS

ALL PURPOSE FLOUR 1 ½ CUPS. ...
BAKING POWDER- 1 ½ TEASPOONS.
EGGS- 4.
SUGAR ALTERNATIVE- 1 ¾ CUPS EQUIVALENT TO SUGAR. ...
BUTTER- 1 ¾ STICKS (¾ CUP) MELTED.
VANILLA EXTRACT- 2 TEASPOONS.
MILK- ½ CUP AND ADDITIONAL (UP TO ¾ CUP TOTAL) IF BATTER SEEMS TOO THICK.

Vanilla muffins are a delicious and healthy dessert that can be easily prepared. With only a few ingredients, you can create a delightful no sugar treat. To start, preheat your oven to 350°F. Then in a bowl, mix together 1 ½ cups all-purpose flour and 1 ½ teaspoons baking powder. In another bowl, whisk together 4 eggs, 1 ¾ cups sugar alternative, and 1 ¾ sticks melted butter. Add 2 teaspoons vanilla extract to the egg mixture. Next, add the wet ingredients to the dry ingredients and mix until combined. If the batter seems too thick, you can add up to an additional ¼ cup of milk. Then pour the batter into a greased muffin tin and bake for 25-30 minutes. Enjoy your delicious and healthy no sugar dessert!

Apple Muffins

With just a few simple ingredients, you can make healthy apple muffins that are perfect for a quick breakfast or snack. Whether you're feeding kids or just looking for an easy-to-make healthy treat, these muffins are sure to be a hit!

To prepare the apple muffins, begin by preheating your oven to 350 degrees Fahrenheit. In a large bowl, combine 2 cups of sugar, 2 eggs, and 1 cup of oil like vegetable, canola, or coconut oil. Then add in 1 tablespoon of vanilla extract. In a separate bowl mix together 3 cups all-purpose flour with 1 teaspoon each of salt, baking soda, and cinnamon. Gradually stir the dry ingredients into the wet ones until both are fully combined.

Fold in 2 cups of diced apples, then spoon the muffin batter into greased or paper-lined muffin tins. Bake the muffins on the center rack in your preheated 350 degree oven for 20 to 25 minutes or until a wooden toothpick inserted into the center comes out clean. Let the muffins cool on a wire cooling rack before serving and enjoy!

The healthy apple muffins are great as a quick breakfast option for kids or as an afternoon snack. They're also delicious served warm with a pat of butter or cream cheese. Make sure to store any leftover muffins in an airtight container at room temperature for up to 4 days. Enjoy!

Strawberry Quinoa Smoothie

This smoothie recipe is perfect for kids and health-conscious adults alike. It's packed with superfoods like quinoa, chia seeds, and wheat germ to give your smoothie a nutrient boost. Here's how to prepare it:

First, gather all the necessary ingredients - 1 large ripe banana, 1 (6 oz) low-fat vanilla Greek yogurt, 1/2 cup cooked quinoa (cooled), 2 Tablespoons honey, 1 Tablespoon chia seeds, 1 Tablespoon wheat germ, 2 cups frozen strawberries (if using fresh, freeze them first), and 1-1/2 cups vanilla almond milk.

Next, add the banana, yogurt, honey, chia seeds, wheat germ and almond milk to a blender. Blend until smooth.

Finally, add the quinoa and frozen strawberries to the smoothie and blend again until smooth. Pour into glasses and enjoy!

This delicious smoothie is healthy, tasty and easy to make - perfect for kids or as a healthy snack for adults. Enjoy!

Sugar Free Brownie

INGREDIENTS

1 EGG.
1 EGG YOLK.
1/2 CUP AVOCADO OIL.
1/2 CUP TRUVIA *
1 TSP VANILLA.
1/3 CUP ALL PURPOSE FLOUR 48G.
1/3 CUP COCOA POWDER 27G.
1/4 TSP SALT.

Sugar Free Brownies are a no-sugar dessert that can be enjoyed by those looking for healthier alternatives. This recipe uses no added sugar, yet still yields delicious and decadent brownies! To prepare this no-sugar dessert, start by preheating your oven to 350 degrees Fahrenheit. Then in a medium bowl, whisk together the egg and egg yolk. Next, pour in the avocado oil and Truvia, whisk until no lumps remain. Add in the vanilla extract and mix well. In a separate bowl, sift together the all-purpose flour, cocoa powder, and salt. Gradually add the dry ingredients to the wet ingredients and stir until no large clumps of flour remain. Grease an 8x8 baking pan with butter and pour in the batter. Bake for 25-30 minutes until a toothpick inserted into the center comes out clean. Allow the brownies to cool before serving, and enjoy this no-sugar dessert! With this recipe, you can indulge in delicious Sugar Free Brownies without the added sugar. Try this no-sugar dessert today and see for yourself how delicious no-sugar desserts can be!

Chocolate Chip Cookies

Making chocolate chip cookies is a fun and easy way to enjoy a no sugar dessert. To begin, preheat your oven to 375°F. Then prepare the ingredients: in a medium bowl, whisk together 2 cups of all-purpose flour, 1 teaspoon of baking soda and ½ teaspoon of salt; set aside. In another large bowl, mix 1 cup of softened butter and the sucralose-granulated sugar blend and sucralose-brown sugar blend together with an electric mixer until they are creamy. After that, add 2 teaspoons of vanilla extract and 2 eggs to the mixture. Beat until everything is combined. Gradually add the flour mixture to the wet ingredients and mix until everything is fully blended.

Finally, fold in your desired amount of chocolate chips into the dough. Drop spoonfuls of dough on an ungreased baking sheet and bake for 10-12 minutes or until golden brown. Let them cool before enjoying this healthy dessert! Enjoy your no sugar cookie masterpiece!

Smoked Salmon Toast

Ingredients
1 ripe avocado.
1 tablespoon crème fraîche.
1 lemon.
70 g radishes.
3 sprigs of fresh dill.
1 tablespoon cider vinegar.
12-16 slices of crispbread or thinly sliced and toasted rye bread.
200 g smoked salmon , from sustainable sources.

Smoked Salmon Toast is a healthy and delicious breakfast option for kids. It's easy to prepare, with just a few simple ingredients - ripe avocado, crème fraîche, lemon, radishes, fresh dill, cider vinegar, crispbread or thinly sliced and toasted rye bread and smoked salmon.

To make the toast: Start by slicing the avocado into thin slices and arranging them on top of the toast. Mix together the crème fraîche with some freshly squeezed lemon juice until combined. Spread this mixture over the avocado slices. Slice the radishes into thin rounds and arrange them around each slice of toast. Sprinkle some finely chopped dill onto each slice of toast. Drizzle over some cider vinegar and top with some smoked salmon.

Serve the Smoked Salmon Toast for a healthy and delicious breakfast for kids. Enjoy!

Kiwi Apple Smoothie

INGREDIENTS

1 SMALL APPLE, PEELED, CUT INTO CHUNKS.
1 KIWIFRUIT, PEELED, CUT INTO CHUNKS.
4 MEDIUM FRESH STRAWBERRIES.
2/3 CUP YOPLAIT® 99% FAT FREE CREAMY STRAWBERRY YOGURT (FROM 2-LB CONTAINER)
1/3 CUP APPLE JUICE.

Kiwi apple smoothie is a great smoothie option for kids. This recipe uses ingredients that are healthy and easy to obtain, making it perfect for busy families. To make the smoothie, start by peeling and cutting an apple into chunks. Place the apple pieces in a blender, followed by one kiwifruit peeled and cut into chunks. Add four medium fresh strawberries, two-thirds cup Yoplait® 99% Fat Free creamy strawberry yogurt from a two-pound container, and one-third cup apple juice. Blend all the ingredients until smooth. Serve immediately for a tasty smoothie with added fruit and protein! Kids will love this smoothie recipe that is both healthy and delicious!

Adding smoothies like the Kiwi Apple smoothie to your family's diet is a great way to ensure that everyone gets the essential vitamins, minerals and nutrients they need. You can also adjust this recipe by adding different flavors of yogurt or juice, depending on your family's tastes. So why not try out this smoothie recipe today? It's sure to be a hit with the whole family!

For smoothie recipes for kids that are both healthy and delicious, look no further than a kiwi apple smoothie. With just a few ingredients and easy instructions, you can create this smoothie quickly and easily. And your kids will love it too!

Apple Chips

If you're looking for a how to prepare no sugar dessert recipe that is both delicious and healthy, look no further than apple chips! The prep time is minimal, and the result is an irresistibly crunchy snack. To make apple chips, preheat your oven to 200°F. Thinly slice your apples, making sure to remove the seeds. Sprinkle them with cinnamon and bake for 1 hour, flipping the apples halfway through the baking time. Let your apple chips cool before indulging in this healthy dessert! Enjoy!

No matter how you choose to prepare your apples, there's no doubt that making a batch of crunchy apple chips is a great way to satisfy your sweet tooth without all the added sugar. With just a few simple ingredients and minimal prep time, you can make this delicious no-sugar dessert recipe in no time! Enjoy your crunchy, healthy snack today!

I want to take a moment to express my heartfelt gratitude for your recent purchase of my recipe book. As a passionate food lover, nothing makes me happier than sharing my favorite recipes with others. Your decision to invest in my book not only supports my dream, but also shows your commitment to expanding your culinary horizons.

I sincerely hope that the recipes in the book will inspire you to try new things and add some excitement to your meals.

Thank you again for your support and for being a part of this journey with me. I hope my book will bring you many happy and delicious moments in the kitchen.

www.ingramcontent.com/pod-product-compliance
Lightning Source LLC
Chambersburg PA
CBHW041151110526
44590CB00027B/4194